D1602003

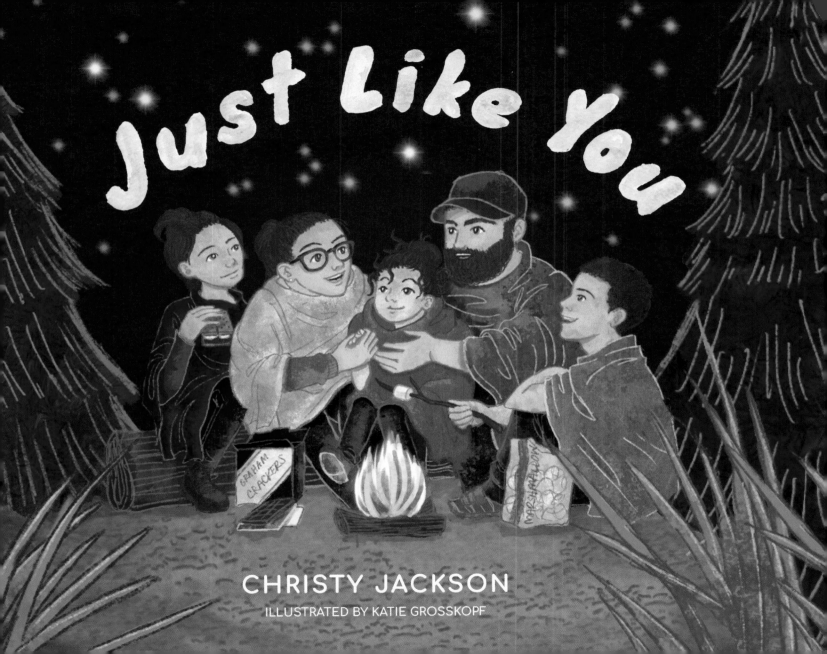

Just Like You

CHRISTY JACKSON

ILLUSTRATED BY KATIE GROSSKOPF

Dedicated to Suzy,
the light in June's life.

And to Grandma Phyllis,
guess what?

I go on fun adventures, just like you.
Camping with my family is my favorite thing to do!

We sit around the fire, making s'mores,
bundling up to stay warm.

Where's your favorite place to explore?

4

Hiking is a special treat!

I like seeing the giant, leafy trees.
Hearing the water rushing through the creek
makes me feel at ease.

Do you enjoy nature, just like me?

We love going to the coast and soaking up the sun.
Days at the beach are so much fun!

Racing across the sand, the wind tickles my face.
I get really excited and giggly — I love this place!

Do you have a favorite park like I do?
I love to swing, just like you.

Mine has extra safety, do you see?
It keeps my wheels from rolling free.

11

When you ride your bike,
I ride my trike.

Isn't it neat
how much we are alike?

12

I can jump really high,
just like a bird in the sky.

But I need strings and springs
to do cool things.

Imagine if we could fly!

When I have a question,
I raise my hand, just like you.

I use buttons to help my friends understand me,
and teachers too.

I like to cuddle with my cat.
He is so fluffy and warm.

He comes to me for lots of snuggles.
When he purrs, I feel calm.

Bath time always makes me laugh!

I sit in my special seat,
kicking the water with my feet.

Do you love splashing too?
I am just like you.

20

We are not so different,
me and you.

I see and feel things,
the same way you do.

When I'm scared,
my mom is there.

When I'm sad,
my dad cares.

And when I'm in a silly mood,
my siblings play along too.

Everyone looks a little different,
and that's what makes us who we ought to be.

26

We all enjoy playing and being included,
kids everywhere, just like you and me.

27

I may not walk, talk, or play
in the same way you do.

But I am happier when we are together,
and having fun, just like you.

28

The end.

About June & Christy

Just Like You is inspired by June Jackson, the fiercest warrior and strongest little girl her mother, author Christy Jackson, has ever known. June was born with a rare genetic disease called Polymicrogyria (PMG). Yet despite her diagnosis, what is most apparent in June is her spirit and love for playing with her siblings and friends.

Christy is a creative writer, advocate for the special needs community, and most importantly, the mother to Addison, Lane, and June. She believes that people of all abilities deserve love, acceptance, and access to fun experiences.

Christy was born and raised in Portland, Oregon, where she lives adventurously with her family. *Just Like You* is her first book.

Sign up for the latest resources and news at:
christyjacksonauthor.com [instagram] @christyajackson